TABLE MOUNTAIN

CARRIE HAMPTON
ANDREW McILLERON

FOREWORD

In the creation story, we are told that when God created the Earth and all living things, he sat back and admired his handiwork, and saw that what he had created was not only good, but very good. Our planet is indeed most beautiful. But when God was busy with his creation, I believe he looked at the southernmost tip of Africa where the two great oceans meet and he said to himself, 'Mmmm... I should do something special here.' And he took the mountains and the oceans and the plants and the animals, and created a southern gateway fitting for the most vibrant, most diverse, most exciting, most wonderful continent in the world.

Now, page by page, this book allows one to muse on the beauty of God's creation, the delightful intricacy of natural design, the reassuring presence of unchanging rock and the fickleness of man. Its authors and designers have balanced

personal creative expression with service to the people of Cape Town by collating the stories and images of this powerful symbol at the heart of the Mother City. Here at last we have a tribute to Hoerikwaggo, Madiba's 'beacon of hope' that rises from the seas as that southern gateway to the great continent.

Desmond M Tutu, Archbishop Emeritus

THE MOUNTAIN OF THE SEA

'Over centuries Table Mountain has stood as a symbol of human capacity for hope and freedom. Whether for the Khoikhoi tribes fighting colonial domination, for Indonesian and Malaysian slaves who for generations have buried their leaders and holy men on its slopes, or for twentieth-century political prisoners. It is a sacred, precious place. To us on Robben Island, Table Mountain was a beacon of hope. It represented the mainland to which we knew we would one day return.' **Nelson Rolihlahla Mandela, former President of South Africa**

Table Mountain is one of the most potent symbols of Africa, and marks the southern entrance to the continent. It is Nelson Mandela's 'beacon of hope', Desmond Tutu's 'southern gateway'. Every Capetonian seems to have an intimate connection with, and affinity for, the iconic landmark, and a story to tell in celebration of the chain of peaks and valleys that runs from Cape Town to Cape Point, as well as the seas that wash against this incredible Peninsula.

The mountain has been a guiding force for centuries and has inspired poetry, art, hymns, legends and even a constellation of stars. According to Nicolaas Vergunst, curator of the *Hoerikwaggo Images of Table Mountain* exhibition at the South African National Gallery in 2001, 'Table Mountain is a multi-layered symbol that speaks through various people in different ways with astonishing clarity, variety and diversity'.

This depth of relationship between the mountain and all who live on or visit her slopes is reflected in the many names by which she is known. Perhaps the most fitting is the original Khoisan name used by the indigenous people of the Cape. They called her, poetically, *Hoerikwaggo* (Mountain in the Sea). And the mountains

do, almost literally, dip their toes straight into the oceans on either side of the long Peninsula. The Khoisan described the whole area as *Camissa* (Place of Sweet Waters) for its clear, fresh streams, which run even in the hot, dry summer. Table Mountain National Park has resurrected the name Hoerikwaggo, both to acknowledge the past and create a link to the present.

A recurring theme in any stories about the mountain is how the past is reflected in the present. Events and characters relating to Table Mountain two or three hundred years ago connect to the present in uncanny ways. Then, as now, life on the mountain slopes included not only hard work and diligence, but drunken driving, duels at dawn, debauched wedding celebrations, pompous officials and women complaining about the wind ruining their hair.

Many people believe that the very structure of Table Mountain holds secrets far older than history. They speak of mysteries such as giant light beings, sun stones, ley lines and the auspicious flow of *qi* (energy). Others repeat the myths and legends that have developed around the mountains and seas when they are at their most treacherous.

PREVIOUS SPREAD Classic Table Mountain – a sight seen by all who sail towards her.
THIS SPREAD The whole length of the Cape Peninsula is visible – from Cape Point to Table Mountain – from a vantage point near Koggelbaai.

THE SHAPE OF THE CAPE

Most other mountains are mere babies compared to Table Mountain, which was formed 260 million years ago during the collision of the Earth's tectonic plates. The Alps and the Himalayas are a tender 32 million and 40 million years old, respectively, and the Rockies a mere 60 million years. Table Mountain has endured the weathering of the ages, and in the process has lost about two-thirds of its original height. It now stands an elegant one kilometre tall, give or take a few metres. Flanked by Devil's Peak on one side and Lion's Head and Signal Hill on the other, Table Mountain presents a stupendous grouping, and must have awed the first humans who wandered this way.

If we leap backward 60 000 years, Cape Town and parts of the South Peninsula were islands, with high points peaking above the water. Then, during glacial periods, when immense quantities of water became solid polar ice caps, the sea level fell as much as 130 m. This resulted in more dry land than we can see today. Between ice ages, the climate warmed up and the ice melted to form islands once again. Evidence of this can be seen from the marine sand that covers about half the Cape Peninsula and all of the Cape Flats. It is upon this sand that many residential suburbs and informal settlements are now located.

In 1830, Charles Darwin visited Cape Town and identified a granite and sedimentary rock contact in Sea Point as being of significant geological importance. He used this to illustrate the molten origin of granite, an idea that ran contrary to the prevailing theory that granite was just another sedimentary rock deposited (like sandstone) as sediment in water. This was a fundamental advance in the understanding of the Earth's geology. On the coastal rocks where Sea Point meets Bantry Bay, it is possible to see that the granite, which started as molten magma, upwelled and forced its way into the older sedimentary rocks, where it cooled and crystallised. The delineation of light igneous granite and the dark sedimentary Malmesbury shale is clearly visible today.

GIANT BOULDERS

Giant granite boulders litter parts of the Cape coastline, and they are particularly noticeable at Boulders Beach, near Simon's Town, where one of only three mainland colonies of African

How high is Table Mountain?

In 1844, at the height of his career, astronomer Sir Thomas Maclear (1794–1879) established a beacon on the highest point of Table Mountain, which still bears his name. He declared the mountain to be 1 085 m high at this point, and this has been its quoted height ever since. However, in 2002 a group of scientists measured it using a Global Positioning System, and proclaimed that the mountain was six metres higher than Maclear's measurement. They had used a theoretical sea level instead of true sea level, and later admitted they were wrong. Their revised height showed that Maclear's original calculation was accurate to within 20 cm.

penguins has taken up residence. At first glance, it would be easy to assume that these boulders must have come tumbling down the mountain – but, in this case, you would be wrong. These boulders have always been where they are. Aeons ago, the hard corestones were topped by softer, weathered granite that was riddled with fractures. Over millions of years, the wetter, more tropical conditions of the very distant past assisted in eroding away the softer granite on top, around the sides and in the fracture joints. All that was left were the enormous rounded boulders that we see today. Given another few million years, and a change from the present dry conditions back to a hotter, damper climate, these boulders could further be worn down and turn to sand. Perceptive visitors with an eye for geological detail will be able to spot this typical granite weathering all over the Peninsula.

INSTANT CHANGE

Millions of years of geological change have little relevance in our everyday life, but the surfers, dog walkers and horse riders of Noordhoek beach can see changes in their environment on a daily basis. This great expanse of beach, six kilometre long and about 250 m wide, is shaped by strong winds, powerful tides, adjoining wetlands and human development. Bordered on one side by the Atlantic, and on the other by a shallow brackish lagoon, the fine white sand of Noordhoek beach may appear almost completely flat after a strong northwesterly wind has levelled it, but within a week it can take on a completely different appearance. Quite suddenly, you will see dune formations a few metres high, with sharply defined ridges and sudden drop-offs where the tide has cut into them. The longer these dunes remain, the more likely they are to become vegetated. But just as the dune grasses

start to take hold, the weather changes and the beach is transformed again. During the winter, a lagoon forms on top of the saturated sand at the edge of the strip of wetland backing the beach, frequently cutting off access to the main part of the beach. At this time, the only way to reach the soft white sand is to hug the little path beside the rocks at the corner known as 'the Hoek', or roll up trouser legs and wade across. But beware: in some places the sand may start to wobble like a jelly – then you know you have hit a patch of quicksand. Once the lagoon has dried up, it forms a long, flat stretch of firm sand. This creates a perfect gallop track for the many horses stabled behind the dunes.

These examples of dramatic change occur within a matter of hours, days or months. Yet Noordhoek provides another amazing example of how the beach has altered

significantly in the past century. The remains of the *Kakapo*, a coal-carrying ship that steamed right up onto the beach by mistake one night in 1900 (see p131), now sit more than 100 m away from the shore. Noordhoek beach is, slowly but surely, growing.

The same cannot be said for other Atlantic coast beaches between Clifton and Sandy Bay. In the past, these were supplemented by sand blown northward along a corridor from Hout Bay, up and over a break in the mountains, to settle and be redistributed into the nearby coves and bays. But construction and land development in the burgeoning Atlantic coast suburbs has seriously restricted this sand movement. If these sands of time cease to move, some of the Peninsula's most popular beaches could eventually disappear.

THIS SPREAD Hout Bay is bordered by the peaks of Karbonkelberg, the Sentinel and Chapman's Peak. *FOLLOWING SPREAD* Sunrise lights up the city's residential suburbs, which climb the slopes of Signal Hill, Lion's Head and Table Mountain.

TABLE MOUNTAIN NATIONAL PARK

Table Mountain National Park (TMNP) is perhaps the most extraordinary park in the world, since its protected natural beauty lies entirely within the greater city limits of Cape Town. It is an urban park that feels like a wilderness. Within minutes of the city centre, you can be in a truly wild place, where only the sounds of nature reach your ears, yet you might have landed on an international flight not even an hour earlier. Table Mountain's peaks are a source of inspiration and beauty, stirring the passions of those who live in its shadow. Such is its importance that TMNP has been declared part of the Cape Floristic Region World Heritage Site.

THE PAST

Table Mountain National Park was created out of a combined effort to bring together, under one management, a diverse collection of nature reserves, institutions and adjoining land belonging to councils and private individuals along the entire Cape Peninsula. This was not an easy task, as nobody wanted to give up his patch or relinquish control.

Perhaps destiny played its part when David Daitz was approached to co-ordinate this project. In his position as Director of Parks and Forests of Cape Town City Council, responsible for Table Mountain and Silvermine Nature Reserves, his view was that the whole mountain chain should be under one authority. Little did he realise that his vociferous opinions were being noted by those who could see the bigger picture. When approached, Daitz realised that his varied background, which included forestry and general management (and not a little stubbornness), were all essential components to enable him to do this ultimate task. He felt this was the job he had been waiting for all his life, and wasn't going to let bureaucrats, politicians, extremists or anybody else prevent him from creating one magnificent park from Cape Town to Cape Point. There were many obstacles and challenges to overcome, and Daitz was given six months to meet rigid conditions set by the Provincial Government of the Western Cape, which, to anyone else, might have seemed insurmountable. He and his team had to get the co-operation of three local authorities (two of whom were initially unwilling) and show significant progress (with no definition of 'significant' or 'progress') in that time.

Daitz believed the outcome would be decided in the court of public opinion rather than by politicians. So, between February and September 1996, he addressed 63 public meetings. He could play a political game if necessary, and he was determined to win. All three local authorities finally signed the land proclamation agreement only a couple of days before a crucial deadline that could have lost the new park a US$12.3 million grant from the Global Environmental Facility.

Daitz realised that he was just a character playing a role at this critical moment, but he had the conviction that the park was meant to be. The process from signature of the land agreements to proclamation of the new national park took just six weeks. Against all odds, his team achieved its objectives, and fulfilled the task that had been asked of it.

The park's Environmental Manager was Howard Langley, who had hitherto looked after nature in preference to working with people. His was the daunting task of establishing a working national park, and with it came a staff of 265 – a turnaround for a man who didn't like people much. At times, it proved to be an overwhelming responsibility. Such was the frenetic pace of operation that he even suffered a minor stroke; but, upon his retirement as Regional Manager of Western Cape National Parks in 2005, he still considered the sacrifices had been worthwhile. He had started his career as a barefoot game ranger in Cape Point Nature Reserve 35 years previously, and had gone full circle. He described it as an extraordinary journey, but for Table Mountain National Park, the journey had just begun.

PREVIOUS SPREAD South Africa's national flower, the king protea.
THIS SPREAD Red Hill moonrise.

When I left South Africa in 1959 by steamship, my last sight of my country was Table Mountain. When I returned 35 years later by plane, the captain swerved to give us a view of Table Mountain and Robben Island. One represented the desolation of oppression, the other the solid, dependable and beautiful face of our country. The mountain's magical qualities continue to haunt, because it encapsulates over thousands of years of our history, from the San and the Khoi, to colonialism and from racism to freedom. **Professor Kader Asmal, MP, former Minister of Education**

THE PRESENT

The formation of a single national park along the entire Cape Peninsula in May 1998 only took place because the right team was in the right place at the right time. The park now extends 60 km from Signal Hill, in the city centre, all the way down the Peninsula to Cape Point. To give it a name recognisable to all people, the citizens of Cape Town voted in February 2004 to change its name from Cape Peninsula National Park to Table Mountain National Park (TMNP).

The Park comprises several sites, some separated by urban areas, others continuous across mountain ranges or linked by beaches, stretches of marshland or sand dunes. Some areas, like the Cape of Good Hope section of the national park, are fenced and charge a conservation fee, which contributes towards the financial sustainability of all 22 of South Africa's national parks.

With approximately 4.2 million visitors to the TMNP each year, serious planning has to go into managing such multitudes of pounding feet. High-usage areas have been protected by the introduction of dedicated paths and boardwalks to minimise damage, and these well-frequented areas cope well, while the rest of the park remains wild and fairly deserted.

TMNP has truly become a park for all people. The young future custodians of our natural heritage are encouraged to climb on the Table Mountain Bus – *iBhasi Yentaba Yetafile* – for a trip up Table Mountain and a Class in the Clouds, or an educational hike along the Hoerikwaggo People's Trail (one of four different Hoerikwaggo Trails, see also pp28, 43).

The Wild Card, on the other hand, gives affordable access to residents and visitors to all of South Africa's national parks. Planning has taken into account all recreational users, including holiday-makers, dog walkers, paragliders, hikers, horse riders, mountain bikers and climbers, and pretty much anybody doing any kind of sport.

As a job creator and labour-intensive employment provider, TMNP provides food for 820 households in the poorest communities along the Park's borders. Temporary employees, such as path builders, firefighters and alien vegetation clearers, supplement the park's 135 or so permanent staff.

PREVIOUS SPREAD Table Mountain rises dramatically out of the urban heart of Cape Town.
THIS SPREAD Cape Point – the south-western tip of Africa. The Victoria & Alfred Waterfront is still a working harbour.

MOUNTAIN WEATHER

Cape Town has what is described as a Mediterranean climate, with hot, dry summers and cool, wet winters. But with a mountain range running down its length and two opposing ocean currents offshore, it also has numerous microclimates and notoriously unpredictable weather. The southeasterly wind, historically named the 'Cape Doctor', swirls against the mountainsides, gathering dust and pollen and giving some people instant hay fever. Luckily, it is possible to escape the worst of this summer wind by retreating to the opposite side of the mountain, where you can bask in calm sunshine. In winter, the northwesterly wind brings rain and storms.

An anonymous 19th century Cape diarist often wrote about the weather and described the effects of a northwester: 'The residents of Camps Bay say that the wind blows with such violence as to pluck their cabbages out of the ground'. She had more to say about the southeaster: 'Oh but this wind is an awful infliction upon Cape Town residents. To venture into the streets while a strong southeaster is blowing, is to expose yourself to ridicule and disgrace, for it is impossible to keep your balance, much less your bonnet!'

TAKE A HIKE

Within half an hour, any visitor or resident of Cape Town can be halfway up a mountain. This is part of what makes Table Mountain National Park so special: it encompasses urbanism and wilderness in the same gust of wind.

The lower slopes are often lush and thick with indigenous protea bushes. The kloofs (ravines) have secret pockets of rare endemic flora and fauna, including orchids found only on Table Mountain. At the top, expansive views take in city, suburbs, ocean, bays and distant mountain ranges. The sense of fulfillment at having climbed this magnificent mountain is enhanced by the knowledge that you can take the cable car down if you have climbed enough for the day.

Table Mountain dominates my life personally and professionally. I work on it, I hike it, I entertain on it. I find it a very strong and calming influence. **John Harrison, Managing Director, Table Mountain Aerial Cableway**

THIS SPREAD *Hout Bay is tucked inside a natural horseshoe of mountains with the Sentinel Peak guarding the entrance.*

FULL MOON ATOP LION'S HEAD

Solitude is not something you should expect if you climb to the top of Lion's Head on full moon night. Reaching the summit for sundown and watching the full moon rising is a Cape Town tradition, and there is always a convoy of Capetonians heading up this short, value-for-effort hike, usually armed with a bottle or can of something refreshing.

It takes only an hour and a half to reach the summit, and the route twirls you around the granite peak, past a magnificent stand of silver trees shimmering in the breeze.

Short but not so sweet for the vertiginous or agoraphobic, this hike does involve a spot of climbing. There is one mandatory ladder climb and another at a steeper part where you can choose between ascending using chains fixed (since 1881) into the rock or continuing along the footpath. Whatever the decision, the short clamber up Lion's Head is worth it, affording sweeping panoramas of Table Mountain, Devil's Peak, the Twelve Apostles, the coastal suburbs and the City Bowl and a limitless vista of the Atlantic Ocean, into which the sun slowly sinks.

The Lion's Head hike provides good opportunities for reflection on contrasts. Civilisation and bustling humanity is so close – the start of the trail is five minutes from the city centre – yet cast your eyes upwards and outwards and the very curve of the Earth becomes visible on the far watery horizon. It is not so hard to imagine why early sailors thought they might fall off the ends of the Earth; from this vantage point you, too, can see where the Earth might end.

HIKING HAZARD

You would think a plant called mountain celery would be a good friend rather than an irritating foe, but its other name is blister bush, and it deserves healthy respect. This plant can inflict very nasty blisters or be completely harmless – it all depends upon the weather conditions. It seems that a compound released onto the skin from the bruised leaves reacts only if exposed to strong sunlight, at which point a dramatic chemical reaction occurs, causing the skin to blister. If the skin is not exposed to ultraviolet rays for a couple of days, blistering shouldn't occur.

Common routes up Table Mountain
(all classed as strenuous)
- **Kasteelspoort** – from Camps Bay
- **Platteklip Gorge** – from Tafelberg Road past the lower cable station
- **Nursery Ravine** – from Kirstenbosch National Botanic Garden
- **Skeleton Gorge** – from Kirstenbosch National Botanic Garden
- **Constantia Corner** – from Cecilia Forest

THIS SPREAD Watching the full moon rise from the top of Lion's Head is a Cape Town tradition.

MARKING THE END OF THE EARTH

Nothing gets the heart pumping more than a good walk by the seaside at Cape Point, in the southernmost part of TMNP. This could be attributed to the energy expended on some of the contours, or quite simply the awesome views of mountain and sea that come together with such force, here at 'the end of the Earth'. Walks around this section of the National Park take in dunes, rock pools, natural springs, coastal and inland vegetation – with the possibility of seeing birds and animals – as well as old signalling cannons and shipwrecks.

For early Portuguese explorers Bartholomeu Dias and Vasco da Gama, who rounded the Cape in 1488 and 1497 respectively, this was a noteworthy enough place to make their mark. It is thought that they placed crosses on this land, as they had done further up the southern African coast. To commemorate the passage of these great sea explorers, two large stone crosses were erected here in the mid-1960s. The crosses serve a secondary purpose, as navigational beacons, lining up with the grave of the old Royal Navy mascot dog, Just Nuisance, to give sailors in False Bay the exact position of submerged Whittle Rock.

Dias had no such beacons to guide him, but he did assist his fellow countrymen by leaving trading materials hidden at the base of each *padrão* (marker cross). Dias must have had a tough time on his journeys; it was he who named the region *Cabo Tormentoso* (Cape of Storms). Later, Portugal's King John gave it the name of *Cabo da Bõa Esperance* (Cape of Good Hope). The sea routes that Da Gama opened up to Asia revolutionised global trade, but also littered the coastline with the wrecks of ships that were unable to round the Cape (see p141).

Global Atmosphere Watch

Because the air at Cape Point is considered to be particularly pure, one of the world's 20 Global Atmosphere Watch (GAW) stations is positioned here. Scientists from the South African Weather Bureau and Germany's Franhofer Institute monitor long-term changes in the chemistry of the Earth's atmosphere. They measure air components, including trace gases such as ozone, carbon dioxide and methane, as well as solar radiation levels, and provide insights into such phenomena as stratospheric ozone depletion and climate change.

THIS SPREAD The land sloping towards Cape Point suggests the end of the Earth is not far.

PAST
AND
PRESENT

The past is particularly evident in the present of Cape Town, even though the city's recorded history goes back little more than 350 years, to the start of European colonisation. However, the indigenous people of the Cape had a knowledge of the mountains and seas that we can only wonder at.

Man is a latecomer to this far tip of land. Not even the Xhosa people, now the majority population in the Cape, were here when Jan van Riebeeck of the Dutch East India Company landed to establish a re-victualling station in 1652. Only the nomadic Khoikhoi herders and San hunter-gatherers lived here; but their impact on the land was minimal, save for grazing a few cattle and sheep and taking food for their immediate needs.

KHOISAN

Khoisan is a generic name used to group two culturally and biologically linked indigenous peoples of southern Africa. The Khoikhoi (also spelled Khoekhoe, and often shortened to Khoi) were nomadic herders who kept domestic herds of sheep and cattle on grasslands watered by the runoff from the mountains. They grazed their herds as long as the pastures could sustain them before moving on. The San (also known as Bushmen), on the other hand, were pure hunter-gatherers, kept no stock and lived only on what the land and sea could provide. To Europeans, they looked alike, and were both referred to as Hottentots (a term considered derogatory). These early inhabitants referred to themselves by their clan names, which for the Khoi included the Cochoqua, Goringhaiqua and Gorachoqua, while Sonqua and Obiqua were typical San tribe names.

The Khoi used to raid each other's *kraals* to steal cattle and marriageable girls. But the San also probably clashed with the Khoi, which is reflected in the names given by the Khoi to some San groups, such as Obiqua and Hawequa, meaning 'murderers'.

The Khoi and San languages were indistinguishable to outsiders, although they varied from clan to clan. Europeans heard nothing but a mouthful of clicks, likening it to the 'clucking of hens'. The European and Khoisan peoples did not understand each other; this was illustrated by an incident in the late 1400s, when the Portuguese explorer Bartholomeu Dias rounded the Cape and landed near Mossel Bay to take on water. The local Khoi defended their water source, and pelted Dias and his men with stones. Permission would probably have been granted, perhaps if politely requested by way of a gift, but the manner in which the Portuguese took the water made the Khoi consider them barbarians. In return, the Portuguese thought the Khoi were savages, semi-naked and putrid-smelling from the mixture of ochre and fat, and sometimes a necklace of intestines, with which they adorned their bodies.

Before the arrival of the Dutch settlers, other European visitors had created the impression that these African aboriginals were cannibals. After living alongside the Khoikhoi for a short while, the Dutch complained about them too – that they devoted themselves to idleness, and neither turned the soil nor spun wool. They found the Khoikhoi ugly, shameless and crude, untrustworthy and thievish, and considered them no better than animals. Within about 70 years of the arrival of European settlers, some Khoisan had retreated to remote parts of the interior and others had been shamelessly exterminated. Today the Southern San Bushmen and Khoikhoi are extinct from the Cape, but their genes live on in much of the population.

Cecil John Rhodes (1853–1902)

Cecil Rhodes was a formidable man who achieved much in his relatively short life. He came to South Africa as a somewhat liberal and open-minded 18-year-old, but was corrupted by wealth and power. He was the founder of the De Beers diamond mining company, Prime Minister of the Cape, acquirer of land in the name of British imperialism and even had a country named after him (Rhodesia). Women who tried to engage Rhodes romantically never had any luck, as he preferred the company of aspiring young men. A statue of Rhodes, in the Company's Gardens in the city centre, shows him pointing north, towards the land between Cape Town and Cairo that he hoped to paint red on the map. To further his vision of imperial federation, Rhodes is said to have structured an Illuminati-like secret society of influential men, the 'Society of the Elect', with an elaborate hierarchical structure. His most enduring legacy is the programme of scholarships awarded annually to deserving students from around the world.

The Old Zoo

Cecil Rhodes wanted to hear the roar of lions in his grand estate, and in 1897 lion cages were built on the upper slopes of the Groote Schuur Estate. These enclosures were replaced by new premises in 1931. Lions were always the main attraction in Rhodes' zoo; they were housed in a raised enclosure with a moat to keep them at a safe distance. Some Cape Town residents can remember hearing the roar of these lions carrying over the suburbs each night at dusk. The zoo was closed in 1975 and many structures were demolished or fell into disrepair. The lion's den survived the passage of time, and has recently been given a new lease of life as an open-air theatre.

THIS SPREAD Summer drought leaves the Rhodes' Estate grasslands on the slopes of Devil's Peak dry and dusty.

was constructed in 1920, and its grand, golden-bricked frontage, heavily draped in ivy, is a classic feature of the mountainside. Groote Schuur Hospital – famous as the site of Dr Christiaan Barnard's first heart transplant in December 1967 – is sited on the northernmost segment of the Groote Schuur Estate, a fact that distressed Rhodes' favoured architect, Sir Herbert Baker (1862– 1946). He predicted that, 'however small now, it is sure to grow, and hospitals have a way of growing like the prickly pear bush, without any symmetry and order'. How true his words proved, and the sprawling hospital complex is situated right opposite the animal-dotted plains across a roaring freeway. Widening of this road and expansion of the university campus, as well as some government buildings, gnawed away at the lower edges of the estate, and its park-like nature was slowly compromised.

Since the estate has come under the control of Table Mountain National Park (TMNP), attempts have been made to interpret the will with Rhodes' aims clearly in mind. These mirror the aims of the national park: a park for the people. However, the realisation of these aims involves a different management process from that applied in the rest of TMNP, since the Groote Schuur Estate contains pastureland and plenty of non-native trees and plants that would normally be removed.

Rhodes preserved the beauty of the land he acquired, but added many imported trees, flowers, birds and animals, the latter kept in large, park-like paddocks. This created a hillside with imposing stands and avenues of great stone pine trees in which sang nightingales, skylarks, thrushes and chaffinches from England. Rhodes added a colourful variety of plants from all over the world, including Brazilian pepper, Spanish broom, Hawaiian hibiscus, Norfolk Island pine, English oak and Pride of India. He stocked his grasslands with African animals like zebra, gemsbok, kudu and springbok, but added kangaroo, wallaby and emu from Australia and llama from Peru. With such a mixed bag of species and the intention of turning this

patch of mountainside into a park, the indigenous vegetation was progressively destroyed, and a folly of nature created within the boundaries of the estate. This transformation cannot wholly be attributed to Rhodes, however, as indigenous people and early settlers contributed to the degradation of the hillside by gathering wood, grazing their livestock and setting fires to clear land for cultivation. Nevertheless, some localised patches of indigenous forest and natural vegetation have survived, providing useful indicators of the plant communities that flourished here in the past.

RHODES MEMORIAL

The most spectacular structure on the estate is Rhodes Memorial. This temple-like stone edifice creates a unique place for reflection, contemplation and meditation, with a wonderful perspective over the city and its surroundings. Rhodes Memorial has exceptional historical importance as a symbolic reference to the life of Cecil Rhodes and his accomplishments – whether you agree with his politics or not. It serves as the primary recreational centre of the estate, and has a popular tea garden. From here, 13 km of paths criss-cross the mountain onto a contour leading to the King's Blockhouse on Mowbray Ridge for expansive views of city and sea.

Built in 1912 to a Sir Herbert Baker design, the memorial is modelled on the unfinished Greek temple at Segesta, in Sicily. Enormous Doric columns set the classical mood. At the top of a broad flight of steps is a large bust of Rhodes, with an inscription by his close friend Rudyard Kipling: 'The immense and brooding spirit still shall quicken and control. Living he was the land, and dead his soul shall be her soul.' You will have to count the number of steps leading to the memorial to know how old Rhodes was when he died. Flanking the steps are eight huge bronze lion statues, similar to those at the foot of Nelson's Column in London's Trafalgar Square.

DISTRICT SIX

THIS SPREAD *Even when modern high-rises block the view of Table Mountain, she appears as a mirror image in their reflective glass.*
FOLLOWING SPREAD *The coastal railway is literally a stone's throw from the sea as it hugs the curve of False Bay from Muizenberg to Simon's Town.*

Nestled below Table Mountain, immediately to the east of the city centre, is the area known as District Six, originally the sixth municipal district of Cape Town. Here lived a vibrant community of freed slaves, merchants, artisans, labourers and immigrants. This mixed society thrived and grew; no doubt District Six had its rougher elements, but former residents recall it as a place of tolerance, where people from different backgrounds got along together.

At the turn of the 20th century, racial marginalisation and forced removals began. The first to be resettled were black Africans, forcibly displaced from the district in 1901. In 1966 District Six was declared a white area, under the terms of the the apartheid government's Group Areas Act, and the life of this community was torn apart. Over the next 16 years, tens of thousands of people were forcibly removed to the windswept, sandy Cape Flats, far from the city centre and their friends and family. Their treasured houses and shops, in the streets where they were born, were bulldozed to the ground. District Six was flattened.

Now District Six is being returned to its original residents, or their sons and daughters. For the most part, the land has lain barren and empty since the removals, save for a scattering of houses, schools and religious buildings that escaped the bulldozers. The land itself seems to bear the bitterness of its history; with the exception of a large technical college, the area was never developed, even though this prime land is within a few minutes' walk of the city centre.

The District Six Museum, located in the old Central Methodist Hall, serves as a reminder of how the area used to be. This museum has broken with traditional ideas of collection and display, and created an interactive public space, with a street map of the district laid out on the floor.

As they walk the lines of the streets they once knew, tears spring to the eyes of former District Six residents. One such former resident, 82-year-old Mr Petersen, was brought to the museum by his daughter, as a surprise. As they paced out the streets, he pointed with his walking stick to the block where he was born. Both became overcome with emotion and wept openly. Another former District Six inhabitant, Dougie Erasmus of Windsor Street, who started the first Latin jazz band in Cape Town, had long refused to visit the desolate site and be forced to relive his memories. It was only when one of the founders of the museum purposely hailed the taxi Dougie drove and asked to be taken to the District Six Museum that he was persuaded to enter it for the first time. There was an old piano, and Dougie could not suppress his desire to play it one last time. The tune he chose? 'They Can't Take That Away From Me.' He died shortly after his visit.

CAPE CARNIVAL

The abolition of slavery in 1834 brought people onto the streets in spontaneous celebrations, marches, music and dancing. This tradition survives in the form of the Cape Carnival, which takes place over several days after New Year. This has become an annual tradition for the Coloured community, and many have no problem referring to its original (though now politically incorrect) name of 'Coon Carnival'. Inspired by American face-painted minstrels, the first organised troupe took to the streets in 1887. Later, the troupes began to compete against each other and their costumes got glitzier and their marching bands slicker. After the forced removals from District Six, the future of the carnival, with its marching brass bands, guitars and banjos, was threatened. It was only in the 1990s that the preferred parade route through town was approved. The Minstrels' Parade is one of the most colourful affairs in Cape Town, and brings the city virtually to a standstill.

FABULOUS FLORA

Fynbos is one of the greatest triumphs of flora, an astounding example of nature's ability to create diversity out of adversity. Fynbos makes up 80% of the Cape Floral Kingdom – the smallest of the world's six floral kingdoms – and comprises some 8 600 species. About two thirds of these are endemic; that is, they are found nowhere else. To put this into perspective, the British Isles, which covers an area three times larger than the Cape Floral Kingdom, has about 1 500 plant species. Table Mountain alone contains more species than this. The Cape Floral Kingdom is tiny in global terms, covering only 90 000 km^2 – about the size of Portugal or Utah – whereas the Boreal Forest Kingdom, which sprawls across the northern continents, covers an area of 50 million km^2.

FIGHTING FIRE

Intervals of 12 to 20 years between fires may sound quite long, but Cape fynbos has adapted to this particular rhythm over thousands of years. This natural rhythm has not yet taken into account the last couple of hundred years, during which time alien vegetation has been introduced. Trees and shrubs brought across from Australia and Europe took root and multiplied so fast that the indigenous fynbos plants were, in places, engulfed by them.

In indigenous fynbos, fire whips through the low foliage and compact bushes in a flash, scorching the earth with low-level heat – just enough for the warmth and smoke to penetrate the earth and encourage the germination of dormant seeds. Fire in alien vegetation is a completely different matter. Australian acacias, commonly called wattles, and including Port Jackson (*Acacia saligna*) and rooikrans (*Acacia cyclops*), have encroached across Cape Town's mountains and coastal belt, and burn with incredible ferocity and intense heat. A fire fuelled by these aliens kills anything in its path.

Even though much of the alien vegetation has been removed, it does not die without a struggle, and often reappears. There are also large areas forested with eucalyptus and pine, which are slowly but surely being eradicated by natural fire, harvesting or national park environmental planning. These species are like tinder to a flame, and a single, thoughtlessly discarded cigarette butt can create a fire that spreads across much of the mountain – as happened in 2006. If the culprit had been around in 1687, he would have been liable to be sentenced to a severe scourging for setting the bush ablaze or, on second offence, hung by a cord until dead.

To extinguish unplanned fires, the authorities call in water-bombing helicopters. The rotor blades of the large Russian Mi-8 helicopters used for firefighting create a distinctive noise, and everyone in Cape Town expects to hear this sound at some point during the summer. Crews of three – two pilots and a flight engineer – are on standby during daylight hours over the summer fire season, and can be operational within minutes. Stationed in a large clearing in Newlands Forest, the giant helicopters rise ominously from between the tall pines, startling motorists on the adjacent highway.

Dangling on a long line below the helicopter is a huge bucket, which can carry 3 000 litres of water. With great precision, the pilot lowers the bucket into the nearest water source, whether it is a lake, a dam or the ocean, and speeds off to drench the fire. The leaping flames at the leading edge of the fire are not what they aim for. They want to chase and dowse the fire from behind; otherwise the blaze will just wrap around the sides of the dampened area and continue unabated.

Clouds of smoke hamper visibility, and the heat of the fire can cause air turbulence. These are added dangers for the pilot, who has to take into account downdrafts from the mountains, and keep steady against the strong winds that push the fire onwards. In addition, he must manage the weight of his bucket, which one moment is full with three tons of water, and the next moment is almost weightless.

ILLEGAL ALIENS

What is considered a friend by one generation is a foe to another, and none more so than trees and shrubs brought to the Cape by its colonisers. Immigrants may have derived short-term benefits, in the form of timber, fodder, dune stabilisation and adornment of their gardens, but the long-term effects on the natural vegetation have been devastating. South Africa has seen thousands of exotic plant species introduced since European mariners and settlers first made landfall on these shores, but the current thinking is that 'aliens must go', and there is even a law against growing certain non-native plants in residential gardens.

In the early 19th century, Lady Anne Barnard commented that many fine trees derived from Australia grew in the Cape and reared their lofty heads from nearly every garden. She praised the good taste and judgement of the governor, Lord Charles Somerset, for planting them. Today, the vast forests of pine and mature old Australian eucalyptus, some planted in Lady Anne's time, are slowly being removed.

The Australian wattles have together proved to be a far greater menace than the thirsty gum and pine trees. They took to the local climate so well that they invaded millions of hectares of land across the Cape, to the terrible detriment of naturally occurring fynbos.

UKUVUKA FIRE STOP CAMPAIGN

Alien clearance has become a priority, and has provided a platform for economic empowerment, providing employment for many who would have struggled to find other work. The Ukuvuka Fire Stop Campaign was born out of the fires that swept across the Cape Peninsula mountains in January 2000. The conflagrations, often fuelled by highly combustible alien vegetation, also burned shacks and houses at the urban edge. Within 10 days of the January 2000 fires, a basic four-year business plan was put in place, funded by sponsorship to the tune of R67.5 million. Six hundred projects were supported, the majority of which involved clearing invasive alien plants or containing fire risk in the National Park and urban areas. Great swathes of green hillsides were cut down, leaving them

---

Extinction by fire

Fires that occur too often in the same place can lead to the extinction of species. The silky-haired pincushion protea and red sugarbush, from the slopes of Lion's Head and Devil's Peak, have both been erased forever. But Burchell's sugarbush, thought to have been extinct, has been rediscovered in the lonely saddle of land between Table Mountain and Devil's Peak.

PREVIOUS SPREAD Table Mountain blazed for several days early in 2006; the fire was started by one carelessly discarded cigarette.
THIS SPREAD (TOP LEFT) Helicopters release 3 000 litres of water per bucket onto runaway fires until the flames subside or darkness falls.
(TOP RIGHT) In a forest-restoration programme, teams are recruited and trained as arboriculturists and chainsaw operators.
(BOTTOM) Only a few trees are still standing the morning after a fire on Signal Hill.

Fire is the most important, rejuvenating, restoring and joyous event in the lifecycle of fynbos. We must break our cycle of ignorance and shock, and prepare ourselves to sit back and enjoy, safely, one of the most amazing spectacles of nature: our fynbos kingdom being rejuvenated – our Phoenix arising: Table Mountain burning! **Tony Rebelo, Scientific Officer, South African National Biodiversity Institute**

Stone pines

These tall, straight pines, with an evergreen canopy, were planted extensively in the 1700s, and Cecil Rhodes planted more on the Groote Schuur Estate (see p66) during the 1890s. With great stature and majesty, the stone pine looks imposing on mountain slopes mostly devoid of large trees. The trees are up to 150 years old, and nearing the end of their natural lives. Other non-native trees pre-dating Rhodes' acquisition of the land include cluster pines, Monterey pines, gum trees and English oaks. An indigenous tree-planting programme in the 1950s inter-planted white stinkwood, Outeniqua yellowwood and Cape ash among the exotics.

Trees & mushrooms

The Tokai Arboretum showcases approximately 1 500 trees of 274 different species, and has been declared a national monument. The forested slopes of the arboretum provide perfect conditions for mushrooms to grow. If you know what you are picking, and are there at the right time on the right day, you may come across richly flavoured porcini mushrooms. But conditions must be just right, and that means being up early after a night of summer rain, with an early sun warming the soil.

PAGES 88–89 Fires started by paraffin stoves in the Joe Slovo township near Cape Town leave people dispossessed and homeless.
PREVIOUS SPREAD Sunrise after the fire: smoke wisps linger around the base of Table Mountain and a fine ash settles on the city.
THIS SPREAD Look up and you may see owls sitting silently on the boughs in Camphor Avenue, Kirstenbosch.

looking brown and bare. After good rains, though, long-forgotten fynbos species poked their heads up and found they had space to grow. Within a year or two, a stunning fynbos landscape began to thrive.

Over the four-year campaign (2000–2004), a complete ring of firebreaks, almost 230 km in extent, was cut to protect the urban edge. Some 5 000 hectares of invasive alien plants were cleared and 164 000 days of work were created. The programme of training and mentoring created 20 new contractors, drawn from four underprivileged communities, each employing a team of 13 previously unskilled workers. The contractors managed their own finance, administration, tendering and workforce. They were entrepreneurs in the making, creating businesses that could stand on their own after the campaign finished.

FROM LITTLE ACORNS

'Mighty oaks from little acorns grow' goes the old adage, but this is not exactly what Table Mountain National Park would like to see. In fact, Park authorities would be happy if they never saw another oak tree. Oaks are not native to South Africa, and were brought here hundreds of years ago when it was fashionable to import flora and fauna. They might have proved useful to the wine industry when fashioned into maturation casks, but the oak trees grew so fast in the ideal conditions of the Cape that the wood became too porous to be useful. This has proven to be positively dangerous on occasion, when sprawling oak boughs have come crashing down without warning.

Pines are also thirsty foreigners, as are the tall Australian eucalyptus trees, which gulp up ground water at an astonishing rate. These fast-growing trees provide straight poles for building and wood pulp for papermaking, and there are still plenty growing in plantations around South Africa. But TMNP does not want them growing on their patch. This creates something of a dilemma, as certain eucalyptus and pine forests have become part of the landscape. Activities such as mountain biking and the family braai are often centred around shady stands of pine and eucalyptus, and it causes a stir when these alien species are removed, and the landscape suddenly looks very different. But within a couple of years, helped by good rainfall, the natural vegetation that had been forced into dormancy bursts forth with abundance, and disgruntled locals are placated.

AFROMONTANE FOREST

The Table Mountain Afromontane forest biome, commonly found below 1 000 m elevation, represents a fraction of what was there thousands of years ago. This is attributed to a change in climate some five million years ago, in which conditions shifted from hot and humid tropical to a Mediterranean rhythm of wet winters and hot, dry summers, with prolonged summer droughts. Fire became a major environmental factor. Although much of the Afromontane forest disappeared, thick patchwork pieces survive in shaded ravines and gorges that have been cut through the rock by mountain streams. Found on the southeastern aspect of Table Mountain, shaded from the hot afternoon sun, they receive far more rainfall than the hot, exposed northwesterly slopes.

As part of the effort to revive indigenous forest, a rehabilitation project is underway in these areas. A seed-collection team hikes into gorges where pockets of glorious Afromontane forest crowd the narrow gullies. They collect precious seeds and bring them to nurseries, where they are grown for a year with minimum intervention. The fine young saplings are then replanted on the mountain. Meanwhile, workers trained in specialist tree-felling techniques enter the gorges and take out the old oaks that will rip holes in the forest canopy when they eventually topple over.

KIRSTENBOSCH NATIONAL BOTANICAL GARDEN

The magnificent setting of Kirstenbosch National Botanical Garden sets it apart from other major botanical gardens. The garden is a floral stage, a botanical theatre that shows off southern Africa's greatest treasures in their natural glory. The Kirstenbosch estate was purchased by Cecil John Rhodes in 1895, as part of his plan to preserve the eastern slopes of Table Mountain for the people of South Africa. On his death in 1902, he bequeathed his estate to the nation (see p66).

Together with getting to the top of Table Mountain, and looking out to sea at Cape Point, a trip to Kirstenbosch is high on the list of priorities for visitors to Cape Town. It is one of those unmissable places. The towering backdrop of Table Mountain plays a pivotal role in creating the tranquil atmosphere of Kirstenbosch. Walking the paths, lawns and hillsides inside the gardens is a soothing experience and should not be hurried. In any case, it is almost impossible to rush around Kirstenbosch;

The air is gentle and silky on the mountains. It seems to engulf you with a sense of peace. I had forgotten how that feels. **Penny Fry, ex-South African resident on holiday from Atlanta, Georgia**

the steep gradients, beautiful flower displays and inviting park benches with sweeping vistas just won't let you.

Take a slow walk up the Camphor Tree Avenue; these trees have taken a hundred years to reach such grand proportions. On their thick boughs it is not uncommon to see large spotted eagle owls, which claim these trees as their own. A little way up the hill is the stage upon which the talented and famous perform on summer Sunday afternoons during the open-air Kirstenbosch Summer Concert series. Behind the grassy slope, where the appreciative audience sits with their picnic baskets, is Jan van Riebeeck's wild almond hedge, planted in 1660 to mark the boundary of the recently established colony, and intended to keep indigenous people from stealing back the sheep and cattle they sold to the settlers.

The many paths that intertwine through the gardens lead visitors through a subtropical arboretum with more than 450 species of trees. Continue past Pearson's Grave, which commemorates the first director of the National Botanical Garden. Professor Pearson was instrumental in establishing the gardens in 1913, and the plaque on his grave is fittingly inscribed, 'If ye seek his monument, look around'.

On the stepped hillside surrounding the oldest part of the gardens, where a dell of tree ferns grow, is an amphitheatre of relics. This arena showcases cycads estimated to be hundreds of years old. These cone-bearing plants were around during the Jurassic Period, between 150 and 200 million years ago, and those that developed heavily spiked fronds were spared being trampled by dinosaurs. Trade in cycads has become a serious problem, and one plant in Kirstenbosch is caged for its own protection. The *Encephalartos woodii* is a male, and no female plant of this type is known to exist. Luckily, it can be propagated from offshoots, so the species does have a future, but the cage is there to stop enthusiasts stealing new side shoots from this singular plant.

At the very top of Kirstenbosch, ericas and proteas bloom to the chirping of long-tailed sugarbirds and sunbirds shot with flashes of electric blue and red, or a shimmering gold. Winter and spring are the seasons to see most proteas at their best, but the rewards of early summer come in a profusion of glorious pincushion proteas, whose orange globes mirror the intensity of an African sunset. On the downhill path, trails lead off to the left to join Smuts' Track, which heads upwards through Skeleton Gorge – a favourite route to the top of Table Mountain. If you decide to venture up the mountain via this track, set aside four hours, and take along a very large bottle of water, a detailed map and good hiking boots. Otherwise, continue to meander through the Fragrance Garden, pinching leaves to release their aromas and learning how to cure any number of ailments.

A CURE FOR ALL

African traditional healers have an intimate knowledge of medicinal herbs and their uses, but their medicines still pose something of a mystery to Europeans. These healers have retained the art of going into the bush and collecting plants, roots and bark to make up lotions and potions that take away toothache and stomach ache, night fevers, bad dreams and even lingering odours.

Many Africans prefer to consult a traditional healer before going to a Western doctor, and it is important that these respected members of society have access to medicinal plants. With funding from the national lottery, a Medicinal Herb Garden has been established on the slopes of Table Mountain near Rhodes Memorial. Healers from the impoverished Cape Flats can come here to learn about soil, plant propagation and sustainable harvesting, and to make sure they have the medicinal plants they need.

Useful tips on plant use can be found in the Fragrance Garden in Kirstenbosch. A specially laid-out trail encourages you to compare textures and sniff a variety of not-always-sweet smells. Zulu women are known to use the fresh-smelling spur sage, ground up and mixed with fat, as a deodorant, while Cape fishermen crush the fine white flowers of the confetti bush to remove fishy odours. You can hang skunk bush from the rafters to keep away flies, or stuff minty *mpephu* into your mattress to remove fleas and lice.

And it is not just the African traditional healers who know what medicines can be harvested from nature. A senior horticulturist at the gardens swears by the sap from mother-in-law's tongue (*Sansevieria trifasciata*), a type of agave, to relieve his children's earaches. Used for centuries in rural villages as a pain reliever, it is also said to cure worms, varicose veins, toothache and piles. The sap of the pig's ear plant (*Cotyledon orbiculata*) will kill your warts with its anti-viral toxins, but it will also kill you if you take a nibble – that is, unless you are a tortoise. They eat it with relish.

The diaries of an anonymous Cape lady, written in the 1860s, reveal an understanding of the medicinal qualities of Cape plants. She wrote, 'The smell of the sugar and buchu bushes, and the pungent odour of the bulbs and African lilies peeping out under their skirts, are the best cures I know for a nervous headache'.

Europe's 10 000 species of plants have been extensively exploited for medicinal purposes, but many of the 21 000 species found in South Africa have yet to be explored for their potential curative properties. So, when visiting Kirstenbosch, don't forget to keep your senses alert; the cure for your earache, headache, varicose veins, worms or warts could be right under your nose.

THIS SPREAD Kirstenbosch Summer Sunset Concerts beneath the castellated peaks of Table Mountain add a powerful element to the experience of listening to music. Every summer Sunday afternoon several thousand people settle themselves on the grassy slope with their picnic baskets.

CREATURES
OF THE
CAPE

Imagine what Cape Town – now populated by several million people – would have looked like before the Europeans arrived. It would have had swathes of red renosterveld grasses, the kind that kept big herds of animals fed. What is now the City Bowl would have been grazed by rhinoceros and buffalo, mountain zebra, hartebeest and eland, and preyed upon by magnificent black-maned Cape lion and secretive leopard. Some kraals would have been created by Khoikhoi pastoralists to protect their sheep and cattle, but they switched their grazing by moving on when pastures became depleted and thus did no lasting damage. In contrast, the sedentary farming style of the colonial period had cattle graze the renosterveld until there was none left. By 1700 there was no thatching grass left and the rhino, buffalo, antelope and lion had moved on or been shot out.

PREVIOUS SPREAD The Cape river frog breeds in deep permanent water.

THIS SPREAD The nature reserve at Cape Point has many ostriches. The black-feathered male sits on his eggs in the dark of night, while the sandy-coloured female takes the day shift.

LET US SUCCEED

In a bold move, one man has brought both rhino and buffalo back to the city. The animals now reside on an **urban conservation reserve** called Solole (meaning 'buffalo'), opposite Masiphumelele township, on the South Peninsula. The township name means 'let us succeed', and Solole keeps this concept firmly in mind.

Solole's owner, Lindsay Hunt, used to supplement his income while he was a student by leading the well-heeled on hunting safaris. But something happened to Hunt to make him change his point of view. In 1999 he found a young springbok that had been abandoned by its mother, and started to bottle-feed it. It slept in his bed and he began to form a bond with the leggy little antelope. As he saw the springbok's personality grow, he realised that every time he shot an animal, he was extinguishing a personality. Soon he was given a baby bontebok, which he named Mnandi, meaning 'wonderful' or 'delicious' (a word used by his tracker whenever he saw a pretty girl). Mnandi was a placid, sweet animal, and Lindsay Hunt became completely enamoured of it. He made a decision never to kill an animal for sport again, and remembered an old hunter-turned-conservationist who had told him, 'Mark my words, by the time you are 30 you will never hunt again'. Until that day, Hunt had thought this was nonsense.

The money he had earned from hunting safaris went into buying a piece of land on which Hunt's orphans could safely live. Hunt let the bush telegraph work its wonders, and soon other orphaned, injured or wild animals in need of a home started arriving. He got bat-eared foxes, genets, owls, grysbok and a tame otter, which he added to his springbok and bontebok to create quite a menagerie. The otter got a touch of wanderlust and crossed a couple of busy roads before winding up, disoriented, in a nearby supermarket car park. Luckily he was lured to safer ground by a female otter living in the wetlands over the hill.

When Hunt became aware of development threats on his boundaries, he bought anything developers were interested in, extending both his overdraft and his reserve, which grew to over 300 hectares. Solole's largest neighbour is now Table Mountain National Park.

The idea of bringing large game back to the Cape occurred to Hunt after he started a buffalo breeding project in the Northern

Province (now Limpopo). Many wild buffalo carry TB, but his breeding herd was disease-free, and this made them highly sought after for game reserves. Hunt made history in 2001 when he brought a few of his favourite buffalo down to his little piece of paradise on the Cape Peninsula. The biggest bull was Silver, a favourite of Hunt's, who had a silver sheen to his coat. He fathered many of Solole's calves before passing away, to be replaced in the hierarchy by Santa. Another beast that holds a special place in Hunt's heart is Tyson, a blind buffalo. Hunt has such a rapport with his animals that he crosses boundaries other people would consider dangerous. After all, buffalo are considered Africa's most dangerous land animal and, when injured, will fight their antagonist to the death.

Hunt made the decision to reintroduce only what had historically occurred in the Cape. He wanted to reintroduce black rhino, an endangered species but, with individual animals costing well over a million rand, this seemed out of reach. But Hunt was not deterred, and didn't stop fundraising until he had enough to buy a young black rhino, Mokwena, who arrived at his new home in December 2004. By the time Mokwena reaches maturity, Hunt hopes to have raised enough money to get him a girlfriend.

Solole Game Reserve provides genuine exposure to urban conservation, where you can see large herbivores in a natural context. Hunt believes conservation will only become important to those who are exposed to it, which is why he thinks that Solole is in exactly the right place – immediately opposite one of Cape Town's poorest communities, where most people live in shacks thrown together from bits of wood and metal. He encourages school groups from the township to come and see the reserve, so that they know what is on the other side of the big wall. Here they can learn conservation aims, and even train to work on the reserve.

The high perimeter wall is there for the protection of both the animals and local residents, as some misguided individuals found out when they scaled it and dropped down into the buffalo enclosure. They either jumped very high to get back over, or were assisted by some buffalo horns. Solole doesn't have much trouble with crime any more.

BROUGHT BACK FROM EXTINCTION

Extinction is forever, or is it? The premise that a species once lost is gone forever has not deterred scientists from undertaking the Quagga Project. The quagga was a local subspecies of the plains zebra that had no stripes on its rump and legs, although its lineage was disputed by a researcher in 1980, who suggested it was more closely related to a horse than a zebra. But since the animal had long passed into extinction – the last one died in Amsterdam Zoo in 1883 – the question of its pedigree seemed merely academic.

The debate about its taxonomic status was settled in 1984. DNA was cloned from four stuffed quagga, one from the South African Museum, and three from the Natural History Museum in Mainz, Germany. Testing confirmed that the quagga was really a subspecies of the plains zebra.

If the quagga was indeed a kind of plains zebra, scientists reasoned that it must be possible to take living zebra with markings characteristic of the quagga, and breed with them to create a quagga-like zebra, at least in external appearance. It is evident from the 23 preserved skins that the quagga displayed great individual colour and pattern variations, but had a distinctive brownish basic stripe colour that faded over the shoulders, and disappeared altogether over the rump. Since the coat pattern was the only criterion by which this subspecies was identified, a new herd with quagga-like coats could justifiably be called quagga.

The first foal, from captured zebras that fitted the bill, was born on 9 December 1988. By July 2004 the Quagga Project had a total of 83 zebras in several herds at different locations, with another six good stallions held in reserve.

In January 2005 the most quagga-like foal so far was born in the selective breeding programme. The stripes on Henry's body (named after the owner of the farm where he was born)

A fishy tale
Imagine the surprise of Table Mountain National Park officials when they were informed, on 30 October 2005, that a two-metre-deep weir on the road leading to and from the lower cableway station was full of fat goldfish – the kind most people keep in a bowl and which most certainly are not native to the mountain streams and dams of Table Mountain. Bewildered officials said they had no idea how the aquatic aliens made the leap from fish tank to cold mountain stream, but thought it must have happened quite recently. Before long, however, reports started coming in from locals that the fish had been there for years. The fishy tale caught the attention of the local press, and a few people reported that they had put goldfish in the stream over the years. One woman said she had taken some of her goldfish to this pool when moving house. TMNP accordingly issued this stern comment: 'We strongly condemn the releasing of alien species into a sensitive ecosystem.' Although there had been no cases of serious invasion by goldfish in South Africa, they constituted an invasive species and had to be removed. There is a happy ending to this story: the fish were transferred to a contained pond near Rhodes Memorial, still on the slopes of Table Mountain and aptly named Mount Pleasant, where they can swim out the rest of their days in bliss.

TAHRS vs KLIPSPRINGERS

Table Mountain is an important biodiversity hotspot, where the balance of nature can easily be upset by species that nature did not intend to be there. A sustained effort is under way to clear alien plants and to remove animals – such as the tahr, a Himalayan mountain goat – that damage the fragile ecology.

For years, the tahrs happily munched fynbos on the rocky slopes of Table Mountain. They were originally brought to the Cape to supplement the collection of animals kept in the old Groote Schuur Zoo (see p68) on the slopes of the mountain near Rhodes Memorial. Goats are master escape artists, and a pair released themselves from their confines and headed off to the mountains to multiply. With no predators or intrusion into their lifestyle, their numbers increased and they led a charmed life.

Goats are notorious for their destructive habits and the damage they can cause, although some would argue that, with an entire mountain on which to graze, a few shaggy goats could do little harm. A difficult and contentious decision was made by SA National Parks management that the tahrs, along with other alien species, had to go.

Eradication of the tahrs has allowed the reintroduction of species that have naturally roamed these mountains in the past. Some nimble klipspringer have successfully been released on Table Mountain after nearly 70 years of local extinction. Their release is a symbol of what the manager of Table Mountain National Park calls 'reconciliation with nature.'

THIS SPREAD Poisonous puff adders inhabit the rocky mountains of the Cape; their excellent camouflage and lazy demeanour can pose a problem as they don't move until trodden on.

FROG FASCINATION

Book publishers never really know what will be a hot seller, and it came as something of a surprise when *Frogs & Frogging*, a field guide to southern African frogs by Vincent Carruthers (published by Struik), turned into a hit. It seems that frogs and toads have fascinated people throughout the ages. Once you learn more about them, it is easy to see why these enigmatic creatures appear in so many stories under a variety of guises.

'Save the Leopard Toad' has become the motto for conservationists in Fish Hoek and Noordhoek, as leopard toads favour the wetlands of these two South Peninsula suburbs. Sturdy and upright, these largest of all southern African toads have distinctive leopard markings in a variety of browns. They are rarely sighted, and when they do emerge to breed, for a few days in August, their presence is announced by loud snoring calls. The leopard toad takes little notice of humans, and may sit on a veranda, 'snoring' (once every three seconds), and refuse to move. Increasing development in this part of the Peninsula not only threatens their habitat, but brings in more cars to squash them on roads and driveways, pushing the leopard toad inexorably towards species endangerment.

The fat, disgruntled-looking rain frog has developed the ability to survive the dry Cape summers by digging itself into soil or leaf litter and only emerging when it rains. One result of this adaptation is that the rain frog has forgotten how to swim. If it lands in a deep puddle, it inflates its grossly rotund body and floats to the edge. Another trick to ensure the survival of its genes is for the male to attach himself to the female's back by secreting a kind of superglue, so strong that no other male can pull him off. The fertilised eggs of the rain frog do not hatch into tadpoles like other frogs; they remain in their jelly capsules until they have metamorphosed into fully developed frogs.

As well as being very rare – only found on an eight-square-kilometre patch of the mountain – the Table Mountain ghost frog is extremely secretive. Few people have ever seen one. The frog keeps away from daylight by resting in narrow cracks in dark caves, and only emerges at night to feed on insects. Camouflage of mud brown and moss green – rather like a combat uniform – equips them perfectly for their preferred habitat of fast-flowing mountain streams and waterfalls. The ghost frog is the product of millions of years of evolution and adaptation, and can climb slippery vertical rock faces using suction pads on its toes. Even winter torrents cannot pry the tadpoles off submerged rocks, thanks to their high-suction mouthparts.

Cape platanna

The rare Cape platanna has an interesting and unfortunate story. This striped, flattened amphibian prefers seasonal lakelets stained the colour of black tea by the acidic mountain soils. Unfortunately, much of its natural habitat has been destroyed by farming and the construction of dams. It also started its own path of self-destruction when it hybridised with the common platanna and the males became sterile. As a result, it has become one of the most endangered amphibians in the world, but can still be found in small, precious pockets known to a select few.

THIS SPREAD *The presence of frogs gives an indication of the health of the environment.*

Know your bird by its call

Attributing a phrase to the sound of a birdcall is a great way to remember which bird makes that particular sound. The fiery-necked nightjar only appears at night among rocky koppies, pleading his poignant message of, 'Good Lord deliver us', while the early-morning Cape turtle dove insists that you 'work harder, work harder.' The hadeda ibis is distinctive for its long, curved beak and dull brown colour, with a shimmer of greenish pink on its shoulder. The hadeda seems to prefer walking to flying, and has a loud, piercing cry. The story goes that these ungainly birds take off from the treetops, and when they look down, they remember they can't fly very well and get a terrible attack of vertigo. So they start screeching, 'Aaaagh, Aaaagh,' until they reach the next treetop or come down to Earth.

THIS SPREAD Seagulls perch on Kalk Bay harbour wall.
FOLLOWING SPREAD There are trails all over the hillsides from which to enjoy vistas such as this one of Red Hill above Scarborough.

WATCHING BIRDS

The Cape may not offer the abundance of colourful birds that are found in the warmer parts of South Africa, but the region is renowned among local and international birders because 42 of South Africa's 53 endemic bird species occur here. For this reason alone, it is worth carrying a pair of binoculars and a bird book when venturing on the mountain.

PREDATORS ON THE WING

The forested slopes and rocky cliffs of the Cape Peninsula are prime raptor-watching areas. Two pairs of black eagles (now renamed Verreaux's eagle) are known to nest on the mountains, and their large, dark silhouettes can be seen gracing the skies along the Peninsula's rugged spine. Hunting co-operatively in pairs, they make low, close passes, swooping silently around rocky outcrops to surprise dassies, which make up part of their diet.

Peregrine falcons are generally rare in South Africa, but are unusually common on Table Mountain. They are masters of the dive, and can reach speeds of up to 380 km per hour to strike their targets, usually small birds. Peregrines share air space with other cliff-nesting species like the rock kestrel, which hunts smaller prey, such as agama and girdled lizards.

Indigenous forests and plantations are the haunts of the agile rufous-chested sparrowhawk and African goshawk. Both species have adapted well to life in wooded suburbia. They surprise their prey by swooping down from concealed positions in the tree canopy. Two buzzards often found in both rural and residential areas are the jackal buzzard and the steppe buzzard. The former is a resident, easily identifiable by its proud rufous chest. The latter is a summer visitor, which undertakes an extraordinary migratory journey from breeding grounds on the steppes of Siberia, other parts of Europe or China. Buzzards feed mostly on rats and mice, as well as doves and the chicks of common game birds such as helmeted guineafowl and Cape francolin (recently renamed Cape spurfowl). Steppe buzzards are welcomed by winemakers, as they arrive just in time to reduce the hordes of rodents that are busy feasting on the sweet grapes ripening in the Cape vineyards.

Black-shouldered and yellow-billed kites are very different in appearance and approach. The black-shouldered kite is a

petite, pale-grey raptor, which can hover gracefully for lengthy periods before dropping onto a mouse or other small rodent. The yellow-billed kite is a large, solidly brown bird with a yellow bill and yellow legs; it will eat just about anything dead or alive. These kites have become so habituated to humans in some parts of southern Africa that they will make passes to steal your lunch or catch food thrown into the air.

The night belongs to owls, in particular the beautiful spotted eagle owl, whose yellow eyes and raised ear tufts give it the familiar 'wise owl' look. An old oak tree or outcrop of inaccessible rock will do as a nesting place for these master hunters of small creatures, particularly nocturnal rodents.

SEABIRDS

Terns, both the Arctic and Antarctic varieties, fly into Cape Town to spend summer and winter, respectively. Those from the Arctic continue on to the Antarctic, so by the time they get back, they have flown around the world from top to bottom and back again. Terns love shallow shorelines and lagoons, such as the one formed on Noordhoek Beach. When disturbed, terns lift as one in a confetti-cloud of fluttering wings, then settle back down once the danger has passed. In addition to terns, the Cape Peninsula is also a good place to see spoonbills, kelp gulls and cormorants.

The black oystercatcher, though one of the rarest of all oystercatchers, is very conspicuous on Cape shores. Its red eyes shine out of a jet black plumage – the only black bird found on the shoreline – and its red beak and legs make it unmistakable. Usually found in pairs, these birds form life-long partnerships and rear a maximum of two chicks once a year. Their existence is threatened because of their habit of laying eggs on exposed sand, where they are walked on or driven over. More than half the world population of black oystercatchers occurs within 300 km of Cape Town, so it is a rare treat to see them.

Further out to sea is the domain of the albatross, and as many as seven species can be seen off the continental shelf. Winter is the best time to see pelagic birds, and a boat trip far out to sea between May and October could reveal 10 000 seabirds of up to 30 different species, such as shearwaters, petrels and prions.

MYTHS, LEGENDS AND THE SACRED MOUNTAIN

Table Mountain has been likened to a fortress, a sleeping goddess, a stairway to heaven, a guardian of the city, a warrior and watcher of the south. It seems to fit all of these descriptions and certainly lends itself to being the central character in many a tale. Many of the Cape's legends are linked with ghosts and apparitions, which you may well see for yourself – with a little imagination, of course. Table Mountain is also considered sacred for the living forces at work behind nature – the invisible behind the visible. The notion that the mountain is somehow sacred is one that many Capetonians would endorse.

THE CLOETES OF ALPHEN

The Cloete family, who sailed to South Africa with Jan van Riebeeck in 1652, became synonymous with the Constantia winelands. Hendrick Cloete owned Groot Constantia, and his great-grandson, Dirk, acquired Alphen in 1860.

The heritage and continuance of the family name was of great importance, so Dirk naturally left the Alphen estate to his son, Henry Cloete. Henry had four daughters, and stipulated that Alphen be left to his eldest grandson, on condition that he took the name Cloete. Nicolette Cloete Bairnsfather gave birth to the first grandchild, a boy named Peter. Tragically, he died in a plane crash while returning from war service in Egypt. Peter's 23-year-old brother, Sandy, inherited Alphen, and against Cloete tradition, left the estate to his eldest daughter, Nicolette. Nicky Cloete-Hopkins now runs Alphen as a commercial venture, with the old manor house used as a hotel and an adjoining room as a well-frequented pub. Each well-worn floorboard and oil painting (including one of Dr James Barry), tells the story of those who have passed through the Alphen estate.

BOER & BRIT

The Anglo-Boer War (1899–1901) tore South Africa asunder and rent families apart. Henry Cloete, although of Dutch descent, was pro-British and acted as a British agent, for which Queen Victoria gave him a medal. Meanwhile his beautiful wife, Christina Deliana van Warmelo, from an old Transvaal family, was passing secrets to Boer agents. In true Victorian style, Deliana supported her husband publicly, but while he dined with British leaders such as Lord Kitchener, she listened carefully and passed this information on via messages secreted in a hollow oak tree. A reply once came in the head of a doll given to daughter Nicolette for Christmas. A photograph shows the three daughters and their dolls, with Nicolette's looking damaged.

Today Alphen is a place where it can be said that Boer and Brit have fully merged. Nicky Cloete, of mixed Dutch and Huguenot descent, married Dudley Hopkins, from British officer stock. Today, they honour both their heritages under the South African flag, which flies over the aptly named Alphen pub, Boer 'n Brit.

Hendrick Cloete

Hendrick Cloete (1725–99) was a demanding man who liked to be woken by a band of fiddlers every morning. His personal slave, August van Bengalen, had to be at his master's side to carry out his every wish. This included holding an extraordinarily long, thin clay pipe while the master smoked it. The attentiveness required from the slave could perhaps have stemmed from the master's immense girth. One visitor ungraciously remarked that he was, 'of such gigantic proportions that if you put him astride one of his own leaguers (a reference to both wine cask and stallion), he would prove a capital Bacchus Africanus.'

THIS SPREAD Hendrina poses with her secateurs during the February grape harvest at Steenberg Wine Estate.

OTHER MOUNTAIN SLOPES

The mountain slopes that stare out to sea along the Atlantic and False Bay coasts are dotted with settlements and villages, all very different but sharing a common engagement with the sea. The rhythmic effects of the waves seem to have a calming effect, and the further south you go, the more relaxed the people become. But it is the sublime city of Cape Town that sets the tone.

CAPE TOWN

Cape Town has grown into an international city, with a potpourri of people from diverse cultural backgrounds living on and around the slopes of Table Mountain. It is African at heart, even though it sometimes doesn't seem very African. Over a period of three and a half centuries, this great city has cultivated a population of 4.7 million. Cape Town's cultural mix is different from the rest of South Africa, drawing from different parts of Europe, southeast Asia, India and Africa. This diversity now characterises the city centre, although most of the towns and villages along the Table Mountain chain embody a more Afro-colonial lifestyle.

A few hundred years ago, Cape Town was a deserted stretch of land, with a scattering of inhabitants who subsisted on what the land and sea provided. After Europeans arrived, the population grew rapidly. The newcomers found fresh water flowing down the slopes of Table Mountain even during the hot, dry summers. These streams fed land fertile enough to support plenty of African grazing animals. But settlers soon changed the landscape and cleared the land to plant grasses suitable for their sheep and cattle. The Dutch East India Company also selected a lovely spot between the sea and the mountain as their central cultivation garden.

As soon as the East India Company ships arrived in 1652, men started tilling the soil in preparation for feeding passing company ships. Their labours were not nearly enough to supply the rapidly growing settlement and passing trade ships, so 300 slaves were put to work in the company's gardens. One third of the fruit and vegetable patch they originally planted remains today as a park in the centre of the city, and is still referred to as the Company's Garden. Oldest of all the plants in the gardens is a steeply leaning saffron pear tree, believed to date from the time of the first settlement. Its main trunk is long dead, but side arms arose around the parent tree, which means this plant has survived for about three and a half centuries. At the lower end of the garden, an oak tree has grown around an old water pump, engulfing it in an arboreal embrace. If the oak tree was there when the pump (dated 1842) was connected, it has taken about 150 years for this tree to swallow the three-metre-high pipe leading to the well below.

One of the main reasons Cape Town became such a successful settlement was the constant supply of sweet water – especially during the hot, dry season – produced through condensation from the 'table cloth' of cloud that forms over Table Mountain. Very early on in the colony, a reservoir was constructed near the Castle, supplying water to the town through *gracht*s (furrows); by 1750, lead pipes directed the water to public fountains.

A stone-lined water furrow ran along the length of the street named Heerengracht (translated from Dutch as 'lords' canal'), where Cape Town's most prosperous residents lived. Pleasant as it was to have watercourses over which little bridges allowed passage, rubbish and even sewage thrown carelessly into them soon created a serious health hazard. By 1850 the *gracht*s had been covered over and even the name of the road had been changed to honour a British parliamentarian, Charles Adderley.

The *gracht*s continued to carry storm water under the roads. The exits and ventilation holes were sealed, but the furrows themselves were never filled in. Some years after gas lighting was introduced in Adderley Street, gas seeped slowly into a great subterranean chamber that had been carved by the underground water. It was lucky there was no spark to ignite this gas – but luck changed when trams were introduced.

At 10.33 am on Tuesday 13 June 1905, workers were installing tram lines along this busy street. One of them, while heating up some metal until it was white-hot, ignited a stream of gas leaking from the underground chamber. Adderley Street quite simply blew up. The ground was ripped open and blue flames burst out of the hissing cracks and fissures. People and horse-drawn cabs disappeared down the holes, or were thrown like rag dolls far across the street. Luckily most cab drivers were spared that day, as a mailship had just arrived in port and cabbies were at the docks waiting for fares.

DAM IT

When the British took over the Cape in the early 1800s, they set about ensuring a more consistent water supply for the city, starting with a dam holding 250 000 gallons. In the first half of the 19th century, the city's water flowed freely, and the fountains overflowed. But by about 1872 it became apparent that the city was on the verge of a water shortage, and households were limited to water for three hours a day.

The city had grown so fast that demands on its water exceeded supply. So began a period of reservoir building, but as each one was finished, demand increased and another had to be built. First came the huge Molteno reservoir in Oranjezicht,

completed in 1886. It became apparent that a tunnel was needed to increase water flow off the mountain and into a pipe, so the Woodhead tunnel was bored 640 m horizontally through raw rock between two buttresses of the Twelve Apostle peaks. Four years later, it was finished. But as a watercourse, it had severe limitations, the exit at Slangolie Ravine being prone to erosion and rock falls, which sometimes also carried off portions of the piping. Many a young Capetonian has been dared to crawl through this tunnel, almost as a rite of passage, but a locked gate now bars the way.

The city council realised that the only way to make a difference to Cape Town's water problems would be a series of reservoirs right on the top of Table Mountain. Thus began the second phase in the story of Cape Town's water, and the first phase in Cape Town's aerial cableway.

Before work could begin on the dams, supplies had to be transported up to the top of the mountain. For this purpose, a cableway was built from Camps Bay. Rising to a height of 695 m in 14 spans, it took 3.7 km of rope to haul up three tonnes of wire for the cables. The first load was sent up in December 1893, and each return journey (including loading and off-loading) took a mere 25 minutes. Sections too heavy to be brought up by the cableway were tied onto wooden sledges and manhandled up the gorge to the working site through the use of block and tackle. Passengers rode up in a precarious-looking open skip. At the summit, a full-scale steam railway was assembled, with tracks laid across the tabletop to haul goods to the works site. The engine is the centrepiece of the Waterworks Museum, located next to the dams on top of the mountain.

CONTACT DETAILS

Table Mountain National Park (TMNP), head office, open 08h00–17h00, Mon–Fri: (021) 701 8692; tablemountain@sanparks.org; www.tmnp.co.za
Wild Cards for multiple entry into National Parks can be bought at any pay gate and many tourist information centres: (086) 123 4002; www.wildinafrica.com
Hoerikwaggo Table Mountain Trail – 3-day luxury, fully portered and catered trail, bookings and information: Patricia Metsing (021) 465 8515; patricia@sanparks.org; www.hoerikwaggotrails.co.za
Table Mountain Aerial Cableway, information line: (021) 424 8181; switchboard (021) 424 0015; www.tablemountain.net; Weatherline: (021) 424 8181
Kirstenbosch National Botanical Garden, open 365 days a year: (021) 799 8800; information desk: (021) 799 8783; www.nbi.ac.za.
Silvertree Restaurant in Kirstenbosch: (021) 762 9585
Photo Hire & Sourcing: (084) 460 7124; (021) 462 6933; fax (021) 461 3880; www.photohire.com; photohire@worldonline.co.za
Free Flight Paragliding Experience: (082) 376 4292; (021) 556 4525; prb@netdial.co.za

TOURISM OFFICES

Cape Town Tourism, city centre bureau: (021) 462 4260;
capetown@tourismcapetown.co.za; www.tourismcapetown.co.za
Cape Town Tourism, V&A Waterfront office: (021) 405 4500
Peninsula Tourism, Simon's Town, open weekdays 09h30–17h30, Saturdays 9h30–13h00, Sundays 10h00–13h00: (021) 786 5790; pensimon@yebo.co.za
Constantia Valley Publicity & Tourism Association: (082) 953 7067; constantiavalley@telkomsa.net; www.constantiavalley.com

ENVIRONMENTAL ORGANISATIONS

Kommetjie Environmental Awareness Group (KEAG): (021) 783 3433; keag@ct.lia.net; www.keag.org.za
Noordhoek Environmental Action Group: (021) 789 1751; www.neag.org.za
Baboon Matters – walks with baboon monitors: (021) 783 3882 or (072) 291 5479; nprm@netactive.co.za
SANCOB bird rescue organisation: (021) 557 6155; info@sanccob.co.za; www.sanccob.co.za

RESCUE SERVICES

Metro Search & Rescue: 10177 (local cellphone network users should dial 112)
Weather Service of South Africa: www.weathersa.co.za
Cape Town International Airport Weather Bureau: (021) 934 0450

BIBLIOGRAPHY

Beyers, CJ et al. 1987. *The Religious Smuts*. Human & Rousseau.

Boonzaier, E, Berens, P, Malherbe, C, Smith, A & Berens, P. 1996. *The Cape Herders*. David Philip.

Bristow, David. 1985. *Mountains of Southern Africa*. Struik Publishers.

Burman, Jose. 1990. *In the Footsteps of Lady Anne Barnard*. Human & Rousseau.

Burman, Jose. 1969. *The Cape of Good Intent*. Human & Rousseau.

Carruthers, Vincent. 2001. *Frogs & Frogging*. Struik Publishers.

Carwardine, Mark. 2003. *Whales Dolphins & Porpoises*. Dorling Kindersley.

Clack, Joy & Mallinick, Catherine. 1998. *Life at the Cape over a Hundred Years Ago*. Struik Publishers.

Coombe, Ed & Slingsby, Peter. 2000. *Place Names in the Cape*. Beard Shaver's Bush.

Dane, Phillippa. 1981. *The Great Houses of Constantia*. Don Nelson.

De Beer, Mona. 1987. *The Lion Mountain*. AA Balkema.

Du Preez, Max. 2004. *Pale Native*. Zebra Press.

Fransen, Hans. 1972. *Groot Constantia – its history and a description of its architecture and collection*. South African Cultural History Museum.

Fuller, Simon Peter. 1994. *Rising out of Chaos – The New Heaven and The New Earth*. Kima Global Press.

Green, Lawrence. 1964. *I Heard The Old Men Say*. Howard Timmins.

Hadithi, Mwenge & Kennaway, Adrienne. *Greedy Zebra*. Picture Knight.

Hampton, Carrie. 2004. *Passport to the Best of Cape Town*. Passport Publications.

Harries, Ann. 1999. *Manly Pursuits*. Bloomsbury.

Hodson, Geoffrey. 1952. *The Kingdom of the Gods*. Theosophical Publishing House.

Jaffer, Mansoor. 1996. *Guide to the Kramats of the Western Cape*. Cape Mazaar (Kramat) Society.

Lundy, Mike. 2006. *Best Walks in the Cape Peninsula* (7th edition). Struik Publishers.

MacPhee, Daniel & de Wit, Maarten. 2004. *How the Cape Got its Shape*. Map Studio.

McIntosh, Fiona & Adey, Shaen. 2004. *Table Mountain Activity Guide*. Struik Publishers.

Miller, Penny. 1979. *Myths & Legends of Southern Africa*. T.V. Bulpin.

Schumann, Dolf & Kirsten, Gerhard. 1995. *Ericas of South Africa*. Timber Press.

Vergunst, Nicolaas. 2000. *Hoerikwaggo Images of Table Mountain*. South African National Gallery.

Webster, Roger. 2002. *At the Fireside*. Spearhead.

Worden, Nigel, van Heyningen, Elizabeth & Bickford-Smith, Vivian. 2004. *Cape Town: The Making of a City*. David Philip.

Yeld, John & Barker, Martine. 2004. *Mountains in the Sea*. SANParks.

INDEX

ACKNOWLEDGMENTS

For sharing their Table Mountain experiences and advice so willingly, I wish to personally thank more people than space allows. I interviewed experts on flora, fauna, geology, history, environment, shipwrecks, hiking, climbing, wine, art, spirituality and mythology. But I started my search for knowledge at the gates of Table Mountain National Park; Brett Myrdal, Fiona Kalk, Howard Langley and David Daitz let me into their world with an insight into the past, present and future of the park. Mike Lundy, Mike Scott, Barry Washkansky, Peter Krige and Ivor Jardine shared their joy of hiking the mountains, and John Harrison of Table Mountain Aerial Cableway unearthed fascinating archive information and got me to the top when I needed a quick fix.

Craig Foster, Dean Liprini, Howard Dobson, Judy Le Cash, Natalia Baker, Antoinette Pedro, Audrey Spronk and Stuart Gedrin revealed their spiritual understandings, and former Mayor Gordon Oliver is still living his message of peace. Artist Robert Slingsby held my attention for hours and master mapmaker Peter Slingsby was a mine of information. Constantia Winelands stories came to light with help from Meri Uribe of Groot Constantia, Sandy Bailey of Steenberg Estate and Nicky Cloete-Hopkins of Alphen. Thanks to Wally Petersen and Glen Ashton for their environmental passion, the ladies of Fish Hoek Museum and Susan de Villiers for knowing all the right people. John Gribble and John Sharfman were invaluable for their shipwreck and lighthouse knowledge, and Sue Kuyper, Callan Cohen and Dr Andrew Jenkins helped me with anything avian. Tony Rebelo and Anthony Hitchcock put me straight on matters of flora, as did Michael Farquhar Curator of Two Oceans on sunfish.

Final thanks to Dominique le Roux, Samantha Menezes-Fick and Lesley Hay-Whitton of Struik.

Carrie Hampton, author

First, I would like to thank my family and friends for their support and encouragement. I would also like to thank Steven Lamb from TMNP, who on many occasions provided invaluable information and put me in contact with the correct people to assist me in getting access to the locations I needed. Also from TMNP I would like to thank Fiona Kalk, Janine Willemans, Paddy Gordon Jannie du Plessis and Nico Olivier; and from TMNP Marine section, Robin Adams, Ralph Kelly, Wille, Riaan and Chris, who took me to sea on the TMNP marine patrol boat, as well as TMNP guides Bongani and Neville.

From Struik, I would like to thank Dominique le Roux, Samantha Menezes-Fick and Lesley Hay-Whitton, who managed and produced and were always a pleasure to work with. Thanks, too, to Pieter and Lauren from Photo Hire; Lennox Mashazu from Cape town disaster management; Sabina Lehman from Table Mountain Aerial Cableway; Ray Muller from Free Flight Paragliding Experience, with whom I flew tandem; and Steve, Doro, Angus and Malcolm for their hospitality; my friends and fellow photographers Steven Goldberg, Mike Story, Andrew Parker, Debra Roets, Alain Proest, Marthinius Hattingh, who from time to time lent me specialist photographic equipment.

Thanks to Denise, Martin and Linda at Hirt & Carter who did the design and repro, and Shaheed and Hendrina who gave me insight into their lives and willingly allowed me to photograph them. Thanks also to Mr Stevenson who organised permissions for me to shoot from a high building in Claremont.

Andrew McIlleron, photographer

First published in 2006 by Struik Publishers
(a division of New Holland Publishing (South Africa) (Pty) Ltd)

New Holland Publishing is a member of Johnnic Communications Ltd

Garfield House
86–88 Edgware Road
W2 2EA London
United Kingdom
www.newhollandpublishers.com

Cornelis Struik House
80 McKenzie Street
Cape Town 8001
South Africa
www.struik.co.za

14 Aquatic Drive
Frenchs Forest
NSW 2086
Australia

218 Lake Road
Northcote
Auckland
New Zealand

ISBN-13: 9 781770 071919
ISBN-10: 1 77007 191 1

1 3 5 7 9 10 8 6 4 2

Publishing manager: Dominique le Roux
Managing editor: Lesley Hay-Whitton
Project co-ordinator: Samantha Menezes-Fick
Designer and map DTP: Martin Jones – Hirt & Carter, Cape
Editors: Helen de Villiers & Alfred LeMaitre
Proofreader: Roxanne Reid
Indexer: Helen de Villiers

Reproduction by Hirt & Carter Cape (Pty) Ltd
Printed and bound by Craft Print International Ltd